MONSTROUS MANNERS

MANNERS ON VACATION

BY BRIDGET HEOS

amicus
illustrated

ILLUSTRATED BY KATYA LONGHI

Amicus Illustrated is published by Amicus
P.O. Box 1329, Mankato, MN 56002
www.amicuspublishing.us

Library of Congress Cataloging-in-Publication Data
Heos, Bridget, author.
 Manners on vacation / by Bridget Heos;
Illustrated by Katya Longhi.
    pages cm. — (Monstrous manners)
 "Amicus Illustrated is published by Amicus."
 Summary: "A young monster with no manners goes
on vacation with her parents and her older sister,
who teaches her how to be polite while traveling and
visiting relatives"— Provided by publisher.
 Audience: K to grade 3.
 ISBN 978-1-60753-747-2 (library binding) —
ISBN 978-1-60753-846-2 (ebook)
 1. Etiquette for children and teenagers. 2. Courtesy–
Juvenile literature. 3. Vacations—Juvenile literature.
 I. Longhi, Katya, illustrator. II. Title.
 BJ1857.C5H466 2016
 395—dc23   2014041498

Editor: Rebecca Glaser
Designer: Kathleen Petelinsek

Printed in the United States of America at
Corporate Graphics in North Mankato, Minnesota.

10 9 8 7 6 5 4 3 2 1

ABOUT THE AUTHOR

Bridget Heos is the author of more than
70 books for children, including *Mustache
Baby* and *Mustache Baby Meets His Match*.
Her favorite manners are holding the door
for others and jumping up to help. You can
find out more about her, if you please, at
www.authorbridgetheos.com.

ABOUT THE ILLUSTRATOR

Katya Longhi was born in southern Italy.
She studied illustration at the Nemo
NT Academy of Digital Arts in Florence.
She loves to create dream worlds with
horses, flying dogs, and princesses in
her illustrations. She currently lives in
northern Italy with her Prince Charming.

Stop, Monster! It's bad manners to run
around in the airport and bump into people.

Mom says to say you're sorry. And sit in time out.
You need to have better manners on vacation, Monster.

Look, it's time to board the plane. Don't
worry, I'll show you how to act politely.

What do you do on the plane? No, Monster. Sit *quietly* and don't bother the other passengers. Find something to do.

Not that! You're kicking the person in front of you! Why don't you read a book, play a game, or look out the window?

It's time to land. How time flies! The flight attendant
is asking you to put your tray up. Listening to the flight
attendant is good manners. It will also keep you safe.

It's time to exit. But wait your turn. The first row goes first, then the second, and so on. I know it's hard to wait, but we have to be patient.

9

EXIT

10

We're here, Monster! What do you do when you see your grandparents?

That's right! You say hello and give them a monster hug.

How can you be a good guest at your grandparents' house? Don't make a mess! Keep your room clean.

Say thank you for the delicious food. And always offer
to help clean up. (But try not to drop the dishes!)

Now, let's go to the beach! The sand is hot. But it's bad manners to step on other people's towels. Wear flip-flops and walk on the sand.

Watch your step! Someone just built that sandcastle. Oops!
Good job saying you're sorry.

It was just an accident. Let's help rebuild the
sandcastle too. It's always good manners to help.

Tonight, we're staying in a hotel. There are lots of other guests here, so no running or yelling in the halls. And no cartwheels either!

Try to get some sleep. Tomorrow we visit . . .

. . . an amusement park! Good
job waiting in line, Monster.

Usually it's not polite to yell unless there is an emergency.
But yelling is okay on a roller coaster!

Good job, Monst—hey, you're not a monster after all. You're my little sister Tiana. And you've learned your manners on vacation. Now, let's go watch a monster movie back at the hotel!

GOOD MANNERS ON VACATION

1. No running in airports, train stations, hotels, or other public places.
2. Sit quietly on a plane, train, or bus.
3. No kicking the seat in front of you.
4. Greet relatives with a smile, handshake, or hug.
5. Keep your room clean when you are a guest.
6. Say thank you for meals.
7. Help your host clean up.
8. At the beach, no throwing sand or stepping on others' things.
9. At hotels, be quiet so you don't bother other guests.
10. Wait nicely in lines.

READ MORE

Brainard, Beth. *Soup Should Be Seen, Not Heard! A Complete Manners Book for Kids*. Bingham, Mass.: Good Idea Kids, 2012.

Ingalls, Ann. *Good Manners in Public*. Mankato, Minn.: Child's World, 2013.

Martineau, Susan. *Respecting Others*. Mankato, Minn.: Smart Apple Media, 2012.

Verdick, Elizabeth. *Don't Behave Like You Live in a Cave*. Minneapolis, Minnesota: Free Spirit Publishing, 2010.

WEBSITES

Can You Teach My Alligator Manners?
disneyjunior.com/can-you-teach-my-alligator-manners
Watch videos and do activities to learn about manners in all different places, including restaurants, playgrounds, and more.

Learn about Manners: Crafts and Activities for Kids
http://www.dltk-kids.com/crafts/miscellaneous/manners.htm
Try these songs, crafts, and coloring pages to learn and practice good manners.

Top Table Manners for Kids
http://www.emilypost.com/home-and-family-life/children-and-teens/408-top-table-manners-for-kids
These table manners apply wherever you eat, on vacation or at someone's house.